INVENTIONS THAT CHANGED THE WORLD

THE TELEVISION

BY SARA GREEN

SmartTV

S	M	T	W	T	F	S	May
					1	2	3
4	5	6	7	8	9	10	
11	12	13	14	15	16	17	
18	19	20	21	22	23	24	
25	26	27	28	29	30	31	

25⁰C

documentary

cinema

concert

search

internet

3D settings

social networks

contents

setup

BLASTOFF!
DISCOVERY

Bellwether Media • Minneapolis, MN

Blastoff! Discovery launches a new mission: reading to learn. Filled with facts and features, each book offers you an exciting new world to explore!

BLASTOFF! UNIVERSE

BLASTOFF! Beginners — GRADE K

BLASTOFF! READERS — GRADES 1-3

BLASTOFF! DISCOVERY — GRADE 4

This edition first published in 2022 by Bellwether Media, Inc.

No part of this publication may be reproduced in whole or in part without written permission of the publisher.
For information regarding permission, write to Bellwether Media, Inc., Attention: Permissions Department,
6012 Blue Circle Drive, Minnetonka, MN 55343.

Library of Congress Cataloging-in-Publication Data

Names: Green, Sara, 1964- author.
Title: The television / by Sara Green.
Description: Minneapolis, MN : Bellwether Media, Inc., 2022. | Series: Blastoff! Discovery: Inventions that changed the world | Includes bibliographical references and index. | Audience: Ages 7-13 | Audience: Grades 4-6 | Summary: "Engaging images accompany information about the invention of the television. The combination of high-interest subject matter and narrative text is intended for students in grades 3 through 8"– Provided by publisher.
Identifiers: LCCN 2021049232 (print) | LCCN 2021049233 (ebook) | ISBN 9781644876176 (library binding) | ISBN 9781648346804 (paperback) | ISBN 9781648346286 (ebook)
Subjects: LCSH: Television–Juvenile literature.
Classification: LCC TK6640 .G74 2022 (print) | LCC TK6640 (ebook) | DDC 621.388–dc23/eng/20211012
LC record available at https://lccn.loc.gov/2021049232
LC ebook record available at https://lccn.loc.gov/2021049233

Text copyright © 2022 by Bellwether Media, Inc. BLASTOFF! DISCOVERY and associated logos are trademarks and/or registered trademarks of Bellwether Media, Inc.

Editor: Rebecca Sabelko   Designer: Josh Brink

Printed in the United States of America, North Mankato, MN.

TABLE OF CONTENTS

PICTURE PERFECT!

Two friends are having a sleepover party! The friend hosting it has a **smart television**. Its **high-definition** technology makes the picture pop. The speaker system fills the room with sound. The TV will add extra fun to the party!

The television is large and thin. It streams hundreds of movies and games and offers millions of songs! The friends can dance to their favorite music, play video games, and watch movies all night long!

The friends decide to play a video game first. They scroll through the game choices and select a racing game. Soon, karts are zooming across the screen. Next, they open a music streaming **app**. They practice new dance moves to their favorite songs!

Later, the friends choose a movie from a movie streaming app. As they settle in to watch it, a parent brings in buttered popcorn. Watching a movie on the large television screen is almost like being at a theater!

TELEVISION BEGINS

Television, or TV, is a technology that sends moving pictures and sounds from one place to another. The pictures and sounds move over wires or through the air as waves of energy.

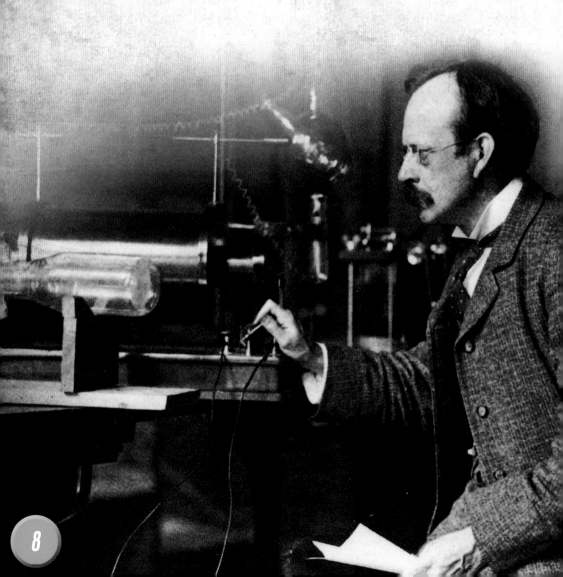

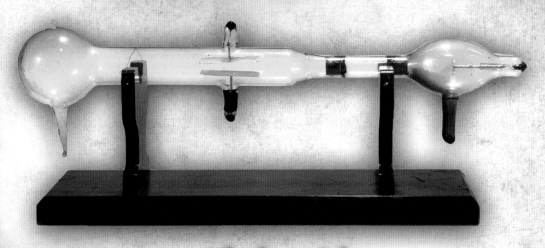

cathode-ray tube

The idea of television was inspired by technology developed in the late 1800s. The telephone and radio showed that **electromagnetic** signals could be sent through the air. An 1897 invention called the **cathode-ray tube**, or CRT, projects electricity through a tube. A spot of light appears at the end of the tube, allowing an image to be made. These developments helped pave the way for television.

An inventor named John Logie Baird created the **mechanical** television in the 1920s. Mechanical televisions used moving parts to capture and show images on screens. Spinning disks had holes cut in a spiral pattern. Light shined through the holes and sent out a signal. They made dim, fuzzy images.

In 1927, Philo T. Farnsworth created the electronic television. It used a CRT to send images to a screen. Electronic televisions showed clearer pictures than mechanical televisions. By 1939, all television **broadcasts** were made for electronic TVs.

DID YOU KNOW?

Philo T. Farnsworth thought of the idea of electronic television at age 14.

John Logie Baird with mechanical television

PIONEER PROFILE

PHILO T. FARNSWORTH

Born:	August 19, 1906, in Beaver, Utah
Died:	March 11, 1971
Background:	Farnsworth was interested in science and technology from a young age. He enjoyed reading science magazines and thinking up inventions.
Invented:	The first all-electronic television system and the picture tube
Year Invented:	1927
Idea Development:	Farnsworth thought mechanical television was too slow. He believed electricity could be used to scan and put images together more quickly. His idea for electronic television was inspired by the plow lines in a field!

early electronic television

11

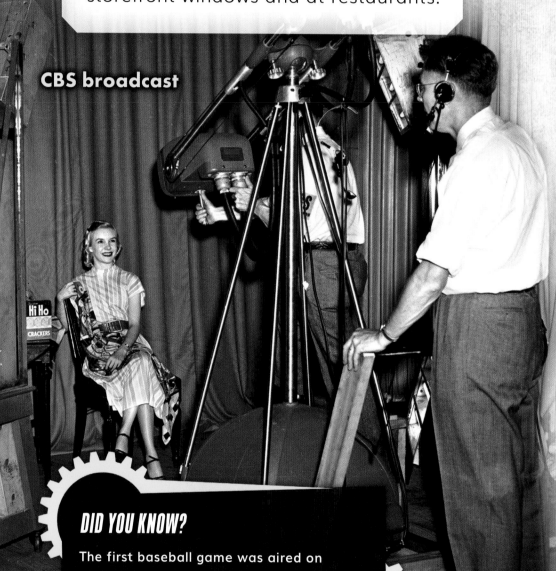

In the 1930s, the NBC and CBS **networks** began broadcasting regular programs. However, televisions were uncommon and expensive. People watched television through storefront windows and at restaurants.

CBS broadcast

DID YOU KNOW?

The first baseball game was aired on television in 1939. The two teams were the Columbia Lions and the Princeton Tigers.

Most television production froze during World War II. But it picked up again after the war ended. In 1946, around 44,000 homes in the United States had a TV set. By the end of 1949, that number had risen to 4.2 million! The number of television networks, stations, and programs also grew. Watching television soon became a part of daily life.

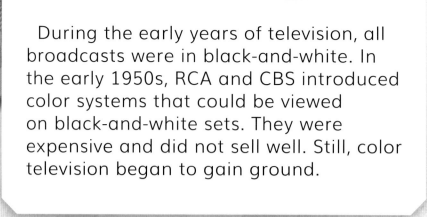

During the early years of television, all broadcasts were in black-and-white. In the early 1950s, RCA and CBS introduced color systems that could be viewed on black-and-white sets. They were expensive and did not sell well. Still, color television began to gain ground.

DID YOU KNOW?

The 1954 Tournament of Roses Parade made history as the first live program to be broadcast in color across the U.S.

CBS color system in 1950

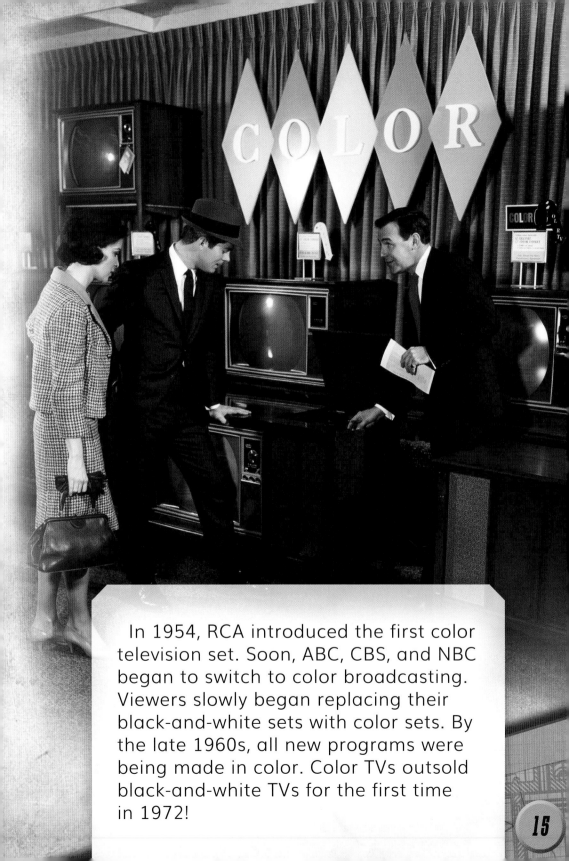

In 1954, RCA introduced the first color television set. Soon, ABC, CBS, and NBC began to switch to color broadcasting. Viewers slowly began replacing their black-and-white sets with color sets. By the late 1960s, all new programs were being made in color. Color TVs outsold black-and-white TVs for the first time in 1972!

Cable television was also on the rise in the early 1970s. The first pay cable network launched in 1972. It was Home Box Office, or HBO. Other cable networks followed, including ESPN in 1979 and The Disney Channel in 1983.

videotapes

VCR

The TV remote control became widely used in the 1980s. Before remotes became popular, people turned a dial on their TVs to change channels. By 1990, many homes also had a **VCR**. People often rented or bought videotapes. They enjoyed watching movies or other taped programs whenever they wanted!

For decades, TV broadcasts only used **analog** signals. Analog signals are made of **radio waves**. They are prone to flickering and **distortion**. Viewers could sometimes see **scan lines** on their screens.

analog signal

HDTV from 2003

Digital broadcasting started in the 1990s. It has better picture and sound quality than analog TV. Digital technology boosted demand for high-definition television, or HDTV. HDTVs have more **pixels** than standard TVs. They make pictures pop. The first HDTVs hit the market in 1998. By the early 2000s, they were top sellers!

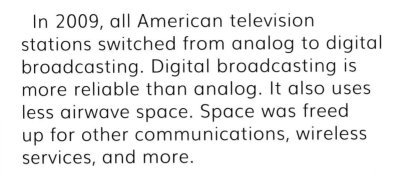

In 2009, all American television stations switched from analog to digital broadcasting. Digital broadcasting is more reliable than analog. It also uses less airwave space. Space was freed up for other communications, wireless services, and more.

DID YOU KNOW?

Viewers who cannot hear well can watch TV with closed captions. Closed captions are words printed on the screen. Viewers can read what is being said on screen.

TV viewing habits changed forever in 2007 when Netflix launched its streaming service. People could watch programs and movies whenever they wanted! Soon, other streaming services became available. Hulu arrived for public streaming in 2008. Disney Plus made its debut in 2019.

GREAT VIEWING!

The 2000s saw a shift from CRT to flat-panel televisions. These either had **plasma** or **LCD** displays. Flat-panel TVs are light and thin and can hang on walls. Their picture quality is crisper, and their screens can be much larger. Around 2010, companies stopped making CRT televisions.

Smart TVs became popular in the 2010s. Smart TVs connect to the Internet and have built-in streaming apps. Many have voice-controlled activation!

smart TV

LIQUID CRYSTAL DISPLAY (LCD) TV

Inventor's Name: An electrical engineer named George Heilmeier led a team of scientists that invented the liquid crystal display in the 1960s.

Year of Release: 1982

How LCD TV Works: LCD TVs are flat-panel televisions. Tiny liquid crystals inside the TV either block light or allow light to pass through them. This creates different colors and brightness levels on the screen.

DID YOU KNOW?

Advances in LCD technology started pushing plasma TVs out of the market around 2007. By 2014, most companies stopped making plasma televisions.

Today, every new TV sold has a flat-panel display. OLED TVs use self-lighting pixels to create richer and brighter colors. QLED TVs use tiny crystals to make crisp pictures!

Screens also continue to get larger. Viewers can feel like they are part of the action. Giant screens can measure 85 inches (215.9 centimeters) or larger! Small TVs are popular, too. They fit easily in kitchens, campers, and other small spaces. People can watch their favorite shows wherever they are!

LCD TELEVISION

2. backlights

4. screen

BREAKING NEWS

1. power supply

3. liquid crystal panel

1. The power supply enters the TV to make energy.
2. Light travels from a large bright backlight from the back of the TV toward the front.
3. The energy causes tiny liquid crystals located inside the TV to move around.
4. The crystals block or let light through in certain ways to make a picture on the screen.

FUTURE SCREEN TIME

Television continues to change in exciting ways. Flexible TV screens roll up and down. Modular TVs have screens that link together. They can be made into different sizes. Other TVs look more like framed photos than television sets!

rollable OLED TV

New lighting technology is making picture color and **contrast** sharper than ever. Some televisions may project **holographic** images into the air. **Virtual reality** TV is also on the horizon. Viewers could step into a show. They might even interact with the characters and plot. Television informs and entertains. It also changes how people view the world!

TELEVISION TIMELINE

1897
Karl Ferdinand Braun invents the cathode-ray tube

1927
Philo T. Farnsworth invents the electronic television

1920s
John Logie Baird makes a mechanical television

1939
NBC begins regularly broadcasting on television in the U.S.

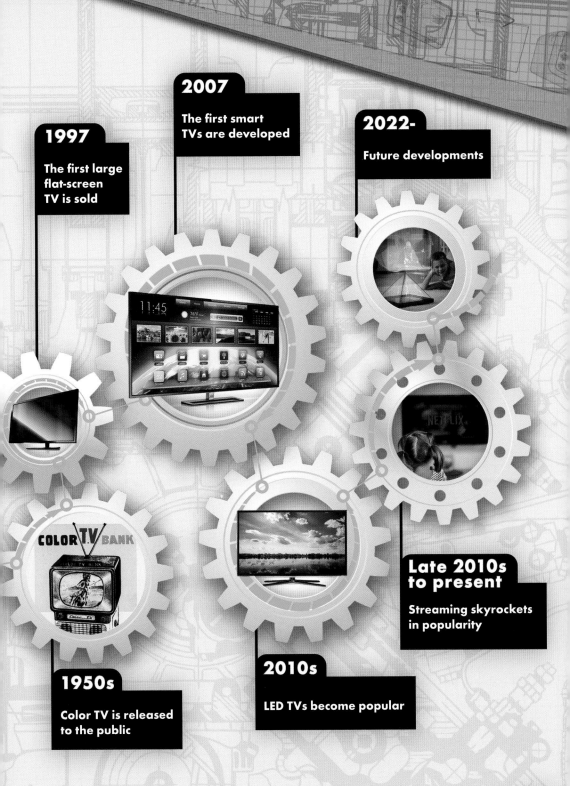

1997

The first large flat-screen TV is sold

2007

The first smart TVs are developed

2022-

Future developments

Late 2010s to present

Streaming skyrockets in popularity

1950s

Color TV is released to the public

2010s

LED TVs become popular

GLOSSARY

analog—related to signals that are continuous

app—a computer program that performs special functions

broadcasts—programs that are sent over television, radio, or the Internet

cathode-ray tube—a glass tube that aims a stream of electricity at a point on a screen

contrast—the difference in color or brightness between different areas

digital—related to signals that send and store information as a series of digits like 1s and 0s

distortion—the state of being twisted out of shape or changing something out of its original form

electromagnetic—related to signals that are able to push or pull something that has an electric charge

high-definition—related to a television system that shows clear, sharp images

holographic—related to images that are three-dimensional

LCD—liquid crystal display; LCD TVs use liquid crystals that use a backlight to produce pictures.

mechanical—made or operated using parts such as levers and gears instead of electronic parts

networks—companies that provide television programming to many television stations

pixels—single points in a picture; each pixel has a color and all the pixels together form a picture.

plasma—a type of gas; plasma TVs use plasma to create a clear picture.

radio waves—invisible waves used to send signals through the air without using wires

scan lines—lines of pixels that create images on a screen when displayed together

smart television—a television connected to the Internet

VCR—videocassette recorder; a VCR is a device used for recording and playing back videotapes.

virtual reality—related to television that allows people to explore a human-made setting

TO LEARN MORE

AT THE LIBRARY

Beevor, Lucy and Marc Tyler Nobleman. *The Invention of the Television*. North Mankato, Minn.: Capstone Press, 2018.

Green, Sara. *The Internet*. Minneapolis, Minn.: Bellwether Media, 2022.

Platt, Charles. *Easy Electronics*. San Francisco, Calif.: Maker Media, 2017.

ON THE WEB

 FACTSURFER

Factsurfer.com gives you a safe, fun way to find more information.

1. Go to www.factsurfer.com.

2. Enter "television" into the search box and click 🔍.

3. Select your book cover to see a list of related content.

INDEX

The images in this book are reproduced through the courtesy of: advent, front cover (hero); Science Museum, London/ Wiki Commons, front cover (small); stefanphotozemun, front cover (schematic left, schematic right); Pixel-Shot, pp. 4-5 (children), 6-7 (children); Andrey_Popov, pp. 4-5 (TV), pp. 6-7 (TV); Pictorial Press/ Alamy, p. 8; Science & Society Picture Library/ Getty Images, p. 9; PA/ Alamy, p. 10; Bettmann/ Getty Images, pp. 11 (Philo T. Farnsworth), 14; Photo Researchers/ Alamy, p. 11 (TV); CBS Photo Archive/ Getty Images, p. 12; Ewing Galloway/ Alamy, p. 13; H. Armstrong Roberts/ClassicStock/ Getty Images, p. 15; Denver Post/ Getty Images, p. 16; Sinisha Karich, p. 17; PitukTV, p. 18 (TV); Homer Sykes/ Alamy, pp. 18 (TV screen), 26; Rick Friedman/ Getty Images, p. 19; Vasyl Shulga, p. 20; pixinoo, p. 21; Proxima Studio, p. 22; begun1983, p. 23; Jasni, p. 24; cobalt88, p. 25 (TV); Lightly Stranded, p. 25 (TV screen); Gorodenkoff, p. 27; Hans Baluschek / Museumsstiftung Post and Telekommunikation/ Wiki Commons, p. 28 (Karl Ferdinand Braun); Library of Congress/ Wiki Commons, p. 28 (John Logie Baird, Philo T. Farnsworth); National Broadcasting Company/ Wiki Commons, p. 28; Buyenlarge / UIG/ Alamy, p. 28 (color TV); BEELDPHOTO, p. 29 (flat screen); Oleksiy Mark, p. 29 (smart TV); Ruslan Ivantsov, p. 29 (LED TV); Morrowind, p. 29 (streaming); Frame Stock Footage, p. 29 (future).